85 Non-Alcoholic Recipes for Home

By: Kelly Johnson

Table of Contents

Beverages
- Virgin Mojito
- Watermelon Mint Cooler
- Ginger Lemonade
- Berry Blast Smoothie
- Iced Hibiscus Tea
- Cucumber Mint Sparkler
- Pineapple Ginger Punch
- Blueberry Lemon Fizz
- Raspberry Lime Spritzer
- Apple Cider Punch

Mocktails
- Nojito (Non-Alcoholic Mojito)
- Virgin Pina Colada
- Shirley Temple
- Virgin Mary
- Mango Tango
- Peach Basil Cooler
- Coconut Pineapple Sparkle
- Kiwi Mint Splash
- Cranberry Orange Spritz

- Grapefruit Rosemary Fizz

Smoothies

- Green Goddess Smoothie
- Tropical Paradise Smoothie
- Peanut Butter Banana Smoothie
- Avocado Spinach Smoothie
- Oatmeal Cookie Smoothie
- Mango Pineapple Bliss
- Chocolate Almond Joy Smoothie
- Blueberry Banana Power Smoothie
- Raspberry Coconut Dream

Iced Teas

- Peach Iced Tea
- Lemon Lavender Iced Tea
- Raspberry Hibiscus Iced Tea
- Minty Mango Iced Tea
- Orange Blossom Iced Tea
- Ginger Peach Iced Tea
- Berry Burst Iced Tea
- Cranberry Apple Iced Tea
- Blueberry Mint Iced Tea
- Chamomile Citrus Iced Tea

Lemonades

- Classic Lemonade
- Strawberry Lemonade

- Lavender Lemonade
- Basil Blueberry Lemonade
- Pineapple GInger Lemonade
- Raspberry Mint Lemonade
- Cucumber Rosemary Lemonade
- Watermelon Basil Lemonade
- Honeydew Mint Lemonade
- Mango Tango Lemonade

Infused Waters

- Cucumber Mint Infused Water
- Strawberry Basil Infused Water
- Citrus Rosemary Infused Water
- Blueberry Lavender Infused Water
- Pineapple Coconut Infused Water
- Watermelon Mint Infused Water
- Kiwi Cucumber Infused Water
- Mango Pineapple Infused Water
- Raspberry Lime Infused Water
- Orange Ginger Infused Water

Hot Drinks

- Apple Cinnamon Hot Toddy (Non-Alcoholic)
- Spiced Chai Latte
- Hot Chocolate Delight
- Golden Turmeric Latte
- Peppermint Hot Cocoa

- Vanilla Rooibos Tea Latte
- Caramel Apple Spice
- Hibiscus Rosehip Tea
- Pumpkin Spice Streamer
- Matcha Green Tea Latte

Beverages

Virgin Mojito

Ingredients:

- 1/2 lime, cut into wedges
- 10 fresh mint leaves
- 2 tablespoons white sugar (adjust to taste)
- 1 cup ice cubes
- 1 cup club soda
- Lime slices and mint sprigs for garnish

Instructions:

Place the lime wedges and mint leaves in a sturdy glass.

Use a muddler or the back of a spoon to gently muddle (mash) the lime and mint together to release the flavors.

Add the white sugar to the glass and muddle a bit more to dissolve the sugar.

Fill the glass with ice cubes.

Pour club soda over the ice and stir gently to mix the ingredients.

Garnish with lime slices and mint sprigs.

Taste and adjust the sweetness by adding more sugar if necessary.

Serve immediately and enjoy your refreshing Virgin Mojito!

Feel free to customize the recipe to suit your taste preferences. Some people like to add a splash of simple syrup for extra sweetness, and you can adjust the mint and lime quantities based on your flavor preferences.

Watermelon Mint Cooler

Ingredients:

- 4 cups fresh watermelon, diced and deseeded
- 1/4 cup fresh mint leaves
- 2 tablespoons honey or agave syrup (adjust to taste)
- 1 tablespoon fresh lime juice
- 2 cups cold water
- Ice cubes
- Mint sprigs and watermelon slices for garnish

Instructions:

In a blender, combine the fresh watermelon, mint leaves, honey or agave syrup, and lime juice.

Blend until smooth and well combined.

Strain the mixture through a fine mesh sieve or cheesecloth into a large pitcher to remove any pulp.

Add cold water to the pitcher and stir well.

Taste the mixture and adjust the sweetness with more honey or agave syrup if needed.

Chill the watermelon mint mixture in the refrigerator for at least 1 hour.

When ready to serve, fill glasses with ice cubes and pour the chilled watermelon mint mixture over the ice.

Garnish with mint sprigs and watermelon slices.

Stir gently before drinking to ensure the flavors are well mixed.

Enjoy your refreshing Watermelon Mint Cooler!

Feel free to get creative and adjust the ingredients to suit your taste preferences. You can also add a splash of sparkling water for some effervescence if you like.

Ginger Lemonade

Ingredients:

- 1 cup freshly squeezed lemon juice (about 4-6 lemons)
- 1/2 cup granulated sugar (adjust to taste)
- 1 tablespoon freshly grated ginger
- 4 cups cold water
- Ice cubes
- Lemon slices and fresh mint for garnish (optional)

Instructions:

In a small saucepan, combine the sugar and grated ginger with 1 cup of water. Heat over medium heat, stirring occasionally, until the sugar completely dissolves. Allow the ginger syrup to cool.

In a large pitcher, combine the freshly squeezed lemon juice with the ginger syrup. Stir well to mix.

Add the cold water to the pitcher and stir again. Taste the lemonade and adjust the sweetness by adding more sugar if necessary.

Chill the ginger lemonade in the refrigerator for at least 1 hour to allow the flavors to meld.

When ready to serve, fill glasses with ice cubes and pour the chilled ginger lemonade over the ice.

Garnish with lemon slices and fresh mint if desired.

Stir gently before serving to ensure the flavors are well combined.

Enjoy your homemade Ginger Lemonade!

Feel free to customize the recipe to your liking. If you prefer a stronger ginger flavor, you can adjust the amount of grated ginger. Similarly, you can tweak the sweetness level to suit your taste buds.

Berry Blast Smoothie

Ingredients:

- 1 cup mixed berries (strawberries, blueberries, raspberries)
- 1/2 cup blackberries
- 1/2 cup plain or vanilla yogurt (Greek yogurt or non-dairy alternative)
- 1/2 cup orange juice
- 1 ripe banana, peeled and sliced
- 1 tablespoon chia seeds (optional)
- 1-2 tablespoons honey or maple syrup (optional, for sweetness)
- Ice cubes (optional)

Instructions:

Place the mixed berries, blackberries, yogurt, orange juice, banana, and chia seeds (if using) in a blender.

Add honey or maple syrup if you desire additional sweetness.

If you prefer a colder and thicker smoothie, you can add a handful of ice cubes.

Blend on high speed until the ingredients are well combined and the smoothie reaches a smooth consistency.

Taste the smoothie and adjust sweetness or thickness if needed.

Pour the Berry Blast Smoothie into glasses.

Optionally, garnish with a few whole berries on top.

Serve immediately and enjoy your delicious and vibrant Berry Blast Smoothie!

Feel free to experiment with the ratio of berries or adjust the sweetness to suit your taste preferences. You can also add other ingredients like spinach for a nutritional boost without altering the flavor significantly.

Iced Hibiscus Tea

Ingredients:

- 2 hibiscus tea bags or 2 tablespoons dried hibiscus petals
- 4 cups water
- 2-3 tablespoons honey or agave syrup (adjust to taste)
- Ice cubes
- Lemon slices or mint leaves for garnish (optional)

Instructions:

Boil 4 cups of water. Once boiled, remove from heat.

Place the hibiscus tea bags or dried hibiscus petals in a heatproof pitcher.

Pour the hot water over the hibiscus tea bags or petals.

Steep the tea for about 5-10 minutes, depending on your desired strength. The longer you steep, the stronger the flavor.

Remove the tea bags or strain out the hibiscus petals.

Stir in honey or agave syrup while the tea is still warm. Adjust the sweetness to your liking.

Allow the tea to cool to room temperature, and then refrigerate for at least 1-2 hours or until chilled.

Fill glasses with ice cubes.

Pour the chilled hibiscus tea over the ice.

Garnish with lemon slices or mint leaves if desired.

Stir gently before serving.

Enjoy your refreshing Iced Hibiscus Tea!

Feel free to customize the recipe by adding other flavors like a splash of orange juice or experimenting with different sweeteners. Iced hibiscus tea is not only delicious but also known for its vibrant red color and potential health benefits.

Cucumber Mint Sparkler

Ingredients:

- 1/2 cucumber, thinly sliced
- 1/4 cup fresh mint leaves
- 1 tablespoon honey or simple syrup (adjust to taste)
- 1 tablespoon fresh lime juice
- 2 cups sparkling water
- Ice cubes
- Cucumber slices and mint sprigs for garnish

Instructions:

In a pitcher, combine the thinly sliced cucumber, fresh mint leaves, honey or simple syrup, and fresh lime juice.

Use a muddler or the back of a spoon to gently muddle (mash) the cucumber and mint to release their flavors.

Add ice cubes to the pitcher.

Pour sparkling water over the ingredients in the pitcher.

Stir the mixture gently to combine the flavors.

Taste and adjust the sweetness by adding more honey or simple syrup if needed.

Pour the Cucumber Mint Sparkler into glasses.

Garnish with cucumber slices and mint sprigs.

Stir gently before serving.

Enjoy your cool and crisp Cucumber Mint Sparkler!

Feel free to customize the recipe by adding a splash of lemon or adjusting the mint and cucumber quantities according to your taste preferences. This drink is not only delicious but also low in calories, making it a healthy and refreshing choice.

Pineapple Ginger Punch

Ingredients:

- 2 cups pineapple juice (freshly squeezed or store-bought)
- 1 cup ginger ale
- 1/4 cup fresh lime juice
- 1/4 cup honey or agave syrup (adjust to taste)
- 1-2 teaspoons freshly grated ginger
- Pineapple slices and mint leaves for garnish
- Ice cubes

Instructions:

In a pitcher, combine the pineapple juice, ginger ale, fresh lime juice, and honey or agave syrup.

Add the freshly grated ginger to the mixture. Adjust the amount according to your preference for ginger flavor.

Stir the punch well to ensure all the ingredients are thoroughly mixed.

Taste the punch and adjust the sweetness or acidity by adding more honey or lime juice if necessary.

Chill the punch in the refrigerator for at least 1-2 hours to enhance the flavors.

Just before serving, add ice cubes to the pitcher and stir gently.

Pour the Pineapple Ginger Punch into glasses.

Garnish each glass with a slice of pineapple and a few mint leaves.

Stir gently before sipping to incorporate the flavors.

Enjoy your tropical and flavorful Pineapple Ginger Punch!

Feel free to get creative and add a splash of sparkling water or club soda for some effervescence. This punch is versatile, and you can adjust the ingredients to suit your taste preferences.

Blueberry Lemon Fizz

Ingredients:

- 1 cup fresh or frozen blueberries
- 2 tablespoons fresh lemon juice
- 2 tablespoons honey or agave syrup (adjust to taste)
- 1 cup sparkling water or club soda
- Ice cubes
- Lemon slices and blueberries for garnish
- Fresh mint leaves (optional)

Instructions:

In a blender, combine the blueberries, fresh lemon juice, and honey or agave syrup.

Blend until you have a smooth blueberry puree.

Strain the blueberry puree through a fine mesh sieve to remove any seeds or pulp.

You can skip this step if you don't mind the texture.

In a glass, add ice cubes.

Pour the blueberry puree over the ice.

Top it off with sparkling water or club soda.

Stir gently to mix the ingredients.

Taste and adjust the sweetness by adding more honey or agave syrup if needed.

Garnish with lemon slices, a few whole blueberries, and fresh mint leaves if desired.

Stir again before drinking to ensure the flavors are well combined.

Enjoy your bubbly and refreshing Blueberry Lemon Fizz!

Feel free to customize the recipe by experimenting with different berries or adding a splash of lemon-lime soda for extra fizziness. Adjust the sweetness to suit your taste, and have fun with this fruity and fizzy concoction!

Raspberry Lime Spritzer

Ingredients:

- 1 cup fresh or frozen raspberries
- 2 tablespoons fresh lime juice
- 2 tablespoons honey or agave syrup (adjust to taste)
- 1 cup sparkling water or club soda
- Ice cubes
- Lime slices and fresh raspberries for garnish
- Mint leaves (optional)

Instructions:

In a blender, combine the raspberries, fresh lime juice, and honey or agave syrup.

Blend until you have a smooth raspberry puree.

Strain the raspberry puree through a fine mesh sieve to remove seeds or pulp. If you prefer a bit of texture, you can skip this step.

In a glass, add ice cubes.

Pour the raspberry puree over the ice.

Top it off with sparkling water or club soda.

Stir gently to mix the ingredients.

Taste and adjust the sweetness by adding more honey or agave syrup if needed.

Garnish with lime slices, a few fresh raspberries, and mint leaves if desired.

Stir again before sipping to ensure the flavors are well combined.

Enjoy your Raspberry Lime Spritzer!

Feel free to customize the recipe by experimenting with different berries or adding a splash of lemon-lime soda for extra fizziness. Adjust the sweetness to suit your taste, and have fun with this fruity and fizzy beverage!

Apple Cider Punch

Ingredients:

- 4 cups apple cider
- 1 cup orange juice
- 1 cup cranberry juice
- 1-2 tablespoons maple syrup or honey (adjust to taste)
- 1 teaspoon ground cinnamon
- 1/2 teaspoon ground nutmeg
- 2 cups ginger ale or sparkling water
- Apple slices and orange slices for garnish
- Cinnamon sticks for garnish (optional)
- Ice cubes

Instructions:

In a large pitcher, combine the apple cider, orange juice, cranberry juice, maple syrup or honey, ground cinnamon, and ground nutmeg.

Stir well to ensure all the ingredients are thoroughly mixed.

Taste the mixture and adjust sweetness or spice levels if needed.

Chill the punch in the refrigerator for at least 1-2 hours to allow the flavors to meld.

Just before serving, add ginger ale or sparkling water to the pitcher and stir gently.

Fill glasses with ice cubes.

Pour the Apple Cider Punch into glasses.

Garnish with apple slices and orange slices.

Optionally, add cinnamon sticks for an extra festive touch.

Stir gently before sipping to incorporate the flavors.

Enjoy your delicious and spiced Apple Cider Punch!

Feel free to get creative and add a splash of lemon or garnish with fresh cranberries for additional color. Adjust the sweetness and spices to suit your taste preferences. This punch is perfect for autumn gatherings or any time you want a comforting and flavorful beverage.

Mocktails

Nojito (Non-Alcoholic Mojito)

Ingredients:

- 10 fresh mint leaves
- 1 tablespoon white sugar (adjust to taste)
- 1 lime, cut into wedges
- 1/2 cup club soda
- Ice cubes
- Mint sprigs and lime slices for garnish

Instructions:

In a glass, muddle the fresh mint leaves, sugar, and a couple of lime wedges.

Muddle gently to release the mint's flavor without breaking it into small pieces.

Fill the glass with ice cubes.

Squeeze the remaining lime wedges into the glass, ensuring the lime juice is well-distributed.

Pour club soda over the ice and lime mixture.

Stir gently to mix the ingredients.

Taste and adjust the sweetness by adding more sugar if needed.

Garnish with mint sprigs and lime slices.

Stir gently before sipping to ensure the flavors are well combined.

Enjoy your refreshing Nojito!

Feel free to customize the recipe to suit your taste preferences. Some people like to add a splash of simple syrup for extra sweetness, and you can adjust the mint and lime quantities based on your flavor preferences. This non-alcoholic version of the Mojito is perfect for those who want a crisp and vibrant drink without the alcohol.

Virgin Pina Colada

Ingredients:

- 1 cup pineapple juice
- 1/2 cup coconut cream
- 1/2 cup crushed ice
- 1 tablespoon granulated sugar (optional, depending on sweetness preference)
- Pineapple slices and maraschino cherries for garnish

Instructions:

In a blender, combine the pineapple juice, coconut cream, crushed ice, and sugar (if using).

Blend on high speed until the mixture is smooth and creamy.

Taste the Piña Colada and adjust sweetness by adding more sugar if needed.

If the consistency is too thick, you can add a little more pineapple juice to reach your desired thickness.

Pour the Virgin Piña Colada into a tall glass.

Garnish with a pineapple slice and a maraschino cherry on top.

Optionally, you can add a small umbrella for a fun tropical touch.

Stir gently before sipping to ensure the flavors are well combined.

Enjoy your Virgin Piña Colada!

Feel free to customize the recipe to suit your preferences. You can also add a splash of lime juice for a bit of tartness or experiment with different types of coconut products, such as coconut milk or coconut water, to achieve the desired level of coconut flavor.

Shirley Temple

Ingredients:

- 1/2 cup ginger ale or lemon-lime soda
- 1/2 cup lemon-lime flavored soda (such as Sprite or 7UP)
- 1 tablespoon grenadine syrup
- Ice cubes
- Maraschino cherry for garnish
- Orange slice for garnish (optional)

Instructions:

Fill a glass with ice cubes.

Pour the ginger ale or lemon-lime soda over the ice.

Add the lemon-lime flavored soda to the glass.

Slowly pour the grenadine syrup over the back of a spoon or by drizzling it down the side of the glass. This helps it settle at the bottom to create the layered look.

Do not stir; let the grenadine settle at the bottom.

Garnish with a maraschino cherry on top.

Optionally, add an orange slice for additional garnish.

Serve with a straw and enjoy your Shirley Temple!

Feel free to adjust the ingredient ratios based on your taste preferences. Some people prefer a sweeter or less sweet version, so you can experiment until you find the perfect balance for you. Shirley Temples are not only delicious but also a fun and nostalgic drink that's enjoyed by people of all ages.

Virgin Mary

Ingredients:

- 1 1/2 cups tomato juice
- 1/2 cup vegetable juice (V8 or similar)
- 1 tablespoon lemon juice
- 1 teaspoon Worcestershire sauce
- 1/2 teaspoon hot sauce (adjust to taste)
- Salt and pepper to taste
- Celery salt for rimming the glass (optional)
- Ice cubes
- Celery stalk and lemon wedge for garnish

Instructions:

If desired, rim the glass with celery salt. To do this, moisten the rim of the glass with a lemon wedge and dip it into celery salt.

Fill the glass with ice cubes.

In a shaker or mixing glass, combine the tomato juice, vegetable juice, lemon juice, Worcestershire sauce, hot sauce, salt, and pepper.

Shake or stir well to mix the ingredients.

Pour the mixture over the ice in the prepared glass.

Garnish with a celery stalk and a lemon wedge.

Optionally, you can add additional garnishes such as olives or pickles.

Stir gently before sipping to ensure the flavors are well combined.

Enjoy your Virgin Mary!

Feel free to customize the recipe to suit your taste preferences. You can adjust the level of spiciness with more or less hot sauce, and add or omit ingredients based on your personal preferences. The Virgin Mary is a versatile and satisfying drink that can be enjoyed at brunch or any time you're in the mood for a savory and spicy non-alcoholic beverage.

Mango Tango

Ingredients:

- 1 cup ripe mango, peeled, pitted, and diced
- 1/2 cup orange juice
- 1 tablespoon lime juice
- 1 tablespoon honey or agave syrup (adjust to taste)
- 1 cup cold water or coconut water
- Ice cubes
- Mango slices and mint leaves for garnish (optional)

Instructions:

In a blender, combine the diced mango, orange juice, lime juice, and honey or agave syrup.

Blend until you have a smooth mango puree.

In a glass, add ice cubes.

Pour the mango puree over the ice.

Add cold water or coconut water to the glass.

Stir gently to mix the ingredients.

Taste and adjust the sweetness by adding more honey or agave syrup if needed.

Garnish with mango slices and mint leaves if desired.

Stir again before sipping to ensure the flavors are well combined.

Enjoy your Mango Tango!

Feel free to get creative with this recipe. You can add a splash of pineapple juice for extra tropical flavor or experiment with different sweeteners. Adjust the thickness by adding more or less liquid, and make it your own refreshing and vibrant Mango Tango!

Peach Basil Cooler

Ingredients:

- 2 ripe peaches, pitted and sliced
- 1/4 cup fresh basil leaves
- 1 tablespoon honey or agave syrup (adjust to taste)
- 1 tablespoon fresh lemon juice
- 2 cups cold water or sparkling water
- Ice cubes
- Peach slices and basil leaves for garnish

Instructions:

In a blender, combine the sliced peaches, fresh basil leaves, honey or agave syrup, and fresh lemon juice.

Blend until you have a smooth peach and basil puree.

Strain the puree through a fine mesh sieve to remove any pulp if desired. This step is optional, and you can skip it if you prefer a bit of texture in your drink.

In a pitcher, combine the peach and basil mixture with cold water or sparkling water.

Stir well to mix the ingredients.

Taste and adjust the sweetness by adding more honey or agave syrup if needed.

Fill glasses with ice cubes.

Pour the Peach Basil Cooler over the ice.

Garnish with peach slices and basil leaves.

Stir gently before serving to ensure the flavors are well combined.

Enjoy your Peach Basil Cooler!

Feel free to customize the recipe to suit your taste preferences. You can add a splash of lime juice for a citrusy kick or experiment with different varieties of basil for unique flavor profiles. This cooler is perfect for warm days and a delightful way to enjoy the flavors of summer.

Coconut Pineapple Sparkle

Ingredients:

- 1 cup pineapple juice
- 1/2 cup coconut milk (full-fat or light)
- 1 tablespoon agave syrup or honey (adjust to taste)
- 1 cup sparkling water or club soda
- Ice cubes
- Pineapple slices for garnish
- Coconut flakes for garnish (optional)

Instructions:

In a glass, combine pineapple juice, coconut milk, and agave syrup or honey.

Stir well to ensure that the ingredients are thoroughly mixed.

Fill the glass with ice cubes.

Pour the sparkling water or club soda over the pineapple and coconut mixture.

Stir gently to combine.

Taste and adjust sweetness by adding more agave syrup or honey if needed.

Garnish with pineapple slices and, if desired, a sprinkle of coconut flakes.

Stir again before sipping to ensure the flavors are well combined.

Enjoy your Coconut Pineapple Sparkle!

Feel free to experiment with the proportions to suit your taste preferences. If you enjoy a stronger coconut flavor, you can add more coconut milk. Likewise, adjust the sweetness to your liking. This tropical drink is perfect for hot days or whenever you're in the mood for a refreshing and bubbly beverage.

Kiwi Mint Splash

Ingredients:

- 2 ripe kiwis, peeled and sliced
- 8-10 fresh mint leaves
- 1-2 tablespoons honey or agave syrup (adjust to taste)
- 1 tablespoon fresh lime or lemon juice
- 2 cups cold water or sparkling water
- Ice cubes
- Kiwi slices and mint sprigs for garnish

Instructions:

In a blender, combine the sliced kiwis, fresh mint leaves, honey or agave syrup, and lime or lemon juice.

Blend until you have a smooth kiwi and mint puree.

Strain the puree through a fine mesh sieve to remove any seeds or pulp if desired.

Alternatively, you can skip this step if you prefer a bit of texture in your drink.

In a pitcher, combine the kiwi and mint mixture with cold water or sparkling water.

Stir well to mix the ingredients.

Taste and adjust the sweetness by adding more honey or agave syrup if needed.

Fill glasses with ice cubes.

Pour the Kiwi Mint Splash over the ice.

Garnish with kiwi slices and mint sprigs.

Stir gently before serving to ensure the flavors are well combined.

Enjoy your Kiwi Mint Splash!

Feel free to customize the recipe to suit your taste preferences. You can add a splash of soda for extra fizziness or experiment with different types of mint for unique flavor profiles. This vibrant drink is not only delicious but also a beautiful and refreshing way to enjoy the flavors of kiwi and mint.

Cranberry Orange Spritz

Ingredients:

- 1/2 cup cranberry juice
- 1/2 cup orange juice
- 1 tablespoon honey or maple syrup (adjust to taste)
- 1 cup sparkling water or club soda
- Ice cubes
- Orange slices and fresh cranberries for garnish
- Mint leaves for garnish (optional)

Instructions:

In a glass, combine the cranberry juice, orange juice, and honey or maple syrup.

Stir well to dissolve the honey or maple syrup.

Fill the glass with ice cubes.

Pour the sparkling water or club soda over the juice mixture.

Stir gently to combine the ingredients.

Taste and adjust sweetness by adding more honey or maple syrup if needed.

Garnish with orange slices and fresh cranberries.

Optionally, add mint leaves for a pop of color and extra freshness.

Stir again before sipping to ensure the flavors are well combined.

Enjoy your Cranberry Orange Spritz!

Feel free to customize the recipe to suit your taste preferences. If you prefer a stronger citrus flavor, you can add more orange juice. Adjust the sweetness to your liking and have fun experimenting with different garnishes. This spritz is perfect for holiday celebrations or any time you want a flavorful and bubbly drink.

Grapefruit Rosemary Fizz

Ingredients:

- 1/2 cup fresh grapefruit juice
- 1 tablespoon rosemary simple syrup (see instructions below)
- 1 cup sparkling water or club soda
- Ice cubes
- Grapefruit slices and fresh rosemary sprigs for garnish

Rosemary Simple Syrup:

- 1/2 cup water
- 1/2 cup granulated sugar
- 2-3 fresh rosemary sprigs

Instructions:

To make the Rosemary Simple Syrup:
- In a small saucepan, combine water, sugar, and rosemary sprigs.
- Bring to a simmer over medium heat, stirring until the sugar is completely dissolved.
- Simmer for 1-2 minutes, then remove from heat and let it cool completely.
- Strain out the rosemary sprigs, leaving you with rosemary-infused simple syrup.

In a glass, combine fresh grapefruit juice and 1 tablespoon of the rosemary simple syrup. Adjust the amount of syrup to your desired sweetness.

Fill the glass with ice cubes.

Pour sparkling water or club soda over the grapefruit and rosemary mixture.

Stir gently to combine the ingredients.

Garnish with grapefruit slices and fresh rosemary sprigs.

Stir again before sipping to ensure the flavors are well combined.

Enjoy your Grapefruit Rosemary Fizz!

Feel free to customize the recipe by adjusting the level of sweetness with more or less rosemary simple syrup. The herbal aroma of rosemary pairs wonderfully with the citrusy brightness of grapefruit, creating a delightful and sophisticated beverage.

Smoothies

Green Goddess Smoothie

Ingredients:

- 1 cup spinach leaves, washed
- 1/2 cucumber, peeled and sliced
- 1/2 avocado, peeled and pitted
- 1/2 banana
- 1/2 cup pineapple chunks (fresh or frozen)
- 1 cup almond milk (or any milk of your choice)
- 1 tablespoon chia seeds (optional)
- Ice cubes (optional)

Instructions:

>Place spinach leaves, cucumber slices, avocado, banana, and pineapple chunks in a blender.
>Add almond milk and chia seeds to the blender.
>If you prefer a colder and thicker smoothie, add ice cubes to the blender.
>Blend on high speed until the ingredients are well combined and the smoothie reaches a creamy consistency.
>Taste the smoothie and adjust sweetness or thickness by adding more banana or pineapple if needed.
>Pour the Green Goddess Smoothie into a glass.
>Optionally, garnish with additional chia seeds, sliced avocado, or a few spinach leaves for a decorative touch.

Stir gently before sipping to ensure the flavors are well mixed.

Enjoy your nutritious and vibrant Green Goddess Smoothie!

Feel free to customize the recipe to your liking. You can add a splash of lime or lemon juice for extra zing or incorporate other greens like kale for variety. This smoothie is an excellent way to pack in essential nutrients while enjoying a delicious and satisfying beverage.

Tropical Paradise Smoothie

Ingredients:

- 1 cup pineapple chunks (fresh or frozen)
- 1/2 cup mango chunks (fresh or frozen)
- 1/2 banana
- 1/2 cup coconut milk
- 1/2 cup orange juice
- 1 tablespoon honey or agave syrup (optional, depending on sweetness preference)
- Ice cubes

Instructions:

In a blender, combine pineapple chunks, mango chunks, banana, coconut milk, and orange juice.

Add honey or agave syrup if you desire additional sweetness.

If you prefer a colder and thicker smoothie, add ice cubes to the blender.

Blend on high speed until the ingredients are well combined and the smoothie reaches a creamy consistency.

Taste the smoothie and adjust sweetness by adding more honey or agave syrup if needed.

Pour the Tropical Paradise Smoothie into a glass.

Optionally, garnish with a slice of pineapple or a wedge of mango on the rim of the glass for a decorative touch.

Stir gently before sipping to ensure the flavors are well mixed.

Enjoy your refreshing Tropical Paradise Smoothie!

Feel free to customize the recipe by adding other tropical fruits such as papaya, kiwi, or passion fruit for a unique twist. Adjust the proportions to suit your taste preferences and enjoy the taste of the tropics in a glass!

Peanut Butter Banana Smoothie

Ingredients:

- 1 banana, peeled and sliced
- 2 tablespoons peanut butter (unsweetened)
- 1 cup milk (dairy or plant-based)
- 1/2 cup plain Greek yogurt
- 1 tablespoon honey or maple syrup (optional, depending on sweetness preference)
- Ice cubes (optional)

Instructions:

In a blender, combine banana slices, peanut butter, milk, Greek yogurt, and honey or maple syrup.

If you prefer a colder and thicker smoothie, add ice cubes to the blender.

Blend on high speed until the ingredients are well combined and the smoothie reaches a creamy consistency.

Taste the smoothie and adjust sweetness by adding more honey or maple syrup if needed.

Pour the Peanut Butter Banana Smoothie into a glass.

Optionally, drizzle a bit of peanut butter on top for extra flavor or garnish with a banana slice.

Stir gently before sipping to ensure the flavors are well mixed.

Enjoy your satisfying and nutritious Peanut Butter Banana Smoothie!

Feel free to customize the recipe based on your preferences. You can add a scoop of protein powder for an additional protein boost or incorporate other ingredients like chia seeds or spinach for added nutrients. This smoothie is not only delicious but also a great way to fuel your day with energy and nutrients.

Avocado Spinach Smoothie

Ingredients:

- 1/2 ripe avocado, peeled and pitted
- 1 cup fresh spinach leaves, washed
- 1/2 banana
- 1/2 cup Greek yogurt (or non-dairy alternative for a vegan version)
- 1 cup almond milk (or any milk of your choice)
- 1 tablespoon chia seeds (optional)
- 1 tablespoon honey or maple syrup (optional, for sweetness)
- Ice cubes (optional)

Instructions:

In a blender, combine the ripe avocado, fresh spinach leaves, banana, Greek yogurt, almond milk, chia seeds (if using), and honey or maple syrup.

If you prefer a colder and thicker smoothie, you can add ice cubes to the blender.

Blend on high speed until the ingredients are well combined and the smoothie reaches a creamy consistency.

Taste the smoothie and adjust sweetness by adding more honey or maple syrup if needed.

Pour the Avocado Spinach Smoothie into a glass.

Optionally, garnish with a few extra spinach leaves on top for a decorative touch.

Stir gently before sipping to ensure the flavors are well mixed.

Enjoy your nutritious and delicious Avocado Spinach Smoothie!

Feel free to customize the recipe based on your preferences. You can also add other ingredients like a squeeze of lime or lemon juice, a handful of berries, or a scoop of protein powder for an extra boost. This smoothie is a great way to incorporate healthy fats, vitamins, and fiber into your diet.

Oatmeal Cookie Smoothie

Ingredients:

- 1/2 cup old-fashioned oats
- 1/2 banana
- 1/4 cup Greek yogurt
- 1 cup almond milk (or any milk of your choice)
- 1 tablespoon almond butter or peanut butter
- 1 tablespoon maple syrup or honey
- 1/2 teaspoon ground cinnamon
- 1/4 teaspoon vanilla extract
- Ice cubes (optional)

Instructions:

In a blender, combine the old-fashioned oats, banana, Greek yogurt, almond milk, almond butter or peanut butter, maple syrup or honey, ground cinnamon, and vanilla extract.

If you prefer a colder and thicker smoothie, you can add ice cubes to the blender.

Blend on high speed until the ingredients are well combined and the smoothie reaches a creamy consistency.

Taste the smoothie and adjust sweetness by adding more maple syrup or honey if needed.

Pour the Oatmeal Cookie Smoothie into a glass.

Optionally, sprinkle a little extra ground cinnamon on top for added flavor.

Stir gently before sipping to ensure the flavors are well mixed.

Enjoy your wholesome and tasty Oatmeal Cookie Smoothie!

Feel free to customize the recipe based on your preferences. You can also add other ingredients like a dash of nutmeg or a handful of raisins for extra oatmeal cookie flavor. This smoothie is not only delicious but also a great way to incorporate oats and healthy ingredients into your diet.

Mango Pineapple Bliss

Ingredients:

- 1 cup ripe mango, peeled and diced
- 1 cup fresh pineapple chunks
- 1/2 banana
- 1/2 cup Greek yogurt (or non-dairy alternative for a vegan version)
- 1/2 cup coconut water or regular water
- 1 tablespoon honey or agave syrup (optional, depending on sweetness preference)
- Ice cubes

Instructions:

In a blender, combine the diced mango, fresh pineapple chunks, banana, Greek yogurt, coconut water (or water), and honey or agave syrup.
If you prefer a colder and thicker smoothie, you can add ice cubes to the blender.
Blend on high speed until the ingredients are well combined and the smoothie reaches a creamy consistency.
Taste the smoothie and adjust sweetness by adding more honey or agave syrup if needed.
Pour the Mango Pineapple Bliss smoothie into a glass.
Optionally, garnish with additional pineapple chunks or a slice of mango for a decorative touch.
Stir gently before sipping to ensure the flavors are well mixed.
Enjoy your tropical and blissful Mango Pineapple smoothie!

Feel free to customize the recipe based on your preferences. You can add a splash of lime or lemon juice for a citrusy kick or incorporate other tropical fruits like papaya or passion fruit. This smoothie is perfect for a quick and delicious taste of the tropics.

Chocolate Almond Joy Smoothie

Ingredients:

- 1 banana
- 1 cup almond milk (or any milk of your choice)
- 2 tablespoons unsweetened cocoa powder
- 2 tablespoons almond butter
- 1 tablespoon shredded coconut (plus extra for garnish)
- 1-2 tablespoons honey or maple syrup (adjust to taste)
- Ice cubes

Instructions:

In a blender, combine the banana, almond milk, cocoa powder, almond butter, shredded coconut, and honey or maple syrup.

If you prefer a colder and thicker smoothie, you can add ice cubes to the blender.

Blend on high speed until the ingredients are well combined and the smoothie reaches a creamy consistency.

Taste the smoothie and adjust sweetness by adding more honey or maple syrup if needed.

Pour the Chocolate Almond Joy Smoothie into a glass.

Optionally, garnish with a sprinkle of shredded coconut on top for added texture.

Stir gently before sipping to ensure the flavors are well mixed.

Enjoy your delicious and chocolatey Almond Joy-inspired smoothie!

Feel free to customize the recipe based on your preferences. You can add a handful of almonds for extra crunch or incorporate a scoop of protein powder for additional protein. This smoothie is a satisfying and sweet treat, perfect for satisfying chocolate and coconut cravings.

Blueberry Banana Power Smoothie

Ingredients:

- 1 cup blueberries (fresh or frozen)
- 1 banana
- 1/2 cup Greek yogurt
- 1 tablespoon almond butter or peanut butter
- 1 tablespoon chia seeds
- 1 cup almond milk (or any milk of your choice)
- 1-2 tablespoons honey or maple syrup (optional, depending on sweetness preference)
- Ice cubes (optional)

Instructions:

In a blender, combine blueberries, banana, Greek yogurt, almond butter or peanut butter, chia seeds, almond milk, and honey or maple syrup.

If you prefer a colder and thicker smoothie, you can add ice cubes to the blender.

Blend on high speed until the ingredients are well combined and the smoothie reaches a creamy consistency.

Taste the smoothie and adjust sweetness by adding more honey or maple syrup if needed.

Pour the Blueberry Banana Power Smoothie into a glass.

Optionally, garnish with a few extra blueberries on top for visual appeal.

Stir gently before sipping to ensure the flavors are well mixed.

Enjoy your nutritious and delicious Blueberry Banana Power Smoothie!

Feel free to customize the recipe based on your preferences. You can add a handful of spinach or kale for added greens, or include a scoop of protein powder for an extra protein boost. This smoothie is not only tasty but also packed with antioxidants, fiber, and protein, making it a great choice for a healthy and energizing drink.

Raspberry Coconut Dream

Ingredients:

- 1 cup fresh or frozen raspberries
- 1/2 cup coconut milk (canned or carton)
- 1/2 banana
- 1/2 cup Greek yogurt (or a non-dairy alternative for a vegan version)
- 1 tablespoon shredded coconut
- 1 tablespoon honey or agave syrup (optional, depending on sweetness preference)
- Ice cubes (optional)

Instructions:

In a blender, combine raspberries, coconut milk, banana, Greek yogurt, shredded coconut, and honey or agave syrup.

If you prefer a colder and thicker smoothie, you can add ice cubes to the blender.

Blend on high speed until the ingredients are well combined and the smoothie reaches a creamy consistency.

Taste the smoothie and adjust sweetness by adding more honey or agave syrup if needed.

Pour the Raspberry Coconut Dream smoothie into a glass.

Optionally, garnish with a sprinkle of shredded coconut on top for added texture.

Stir gently before sipping to ensure the flavors are well mixed.

Enjoy your tropical and flavorful Raspberry Coconut Dream!

Feel free to customize the recipe based on your preferences. You can add a splash of lime juice for a citrusy twist or include a handful of spinach for an extra nutritional boost. This smoothie is not only delicious but also a fantastic way to enjoy the combined goodness of raspberries and coconut.

Iced Teas

Peach Iced Tea

Ingredients:

- 4-5 ripe peaches, pitted and sliced (fresh or frozen)
- 4 cups water
- 4-6 black tea bags
- 1/2 cup sugar (adjust to taste)
- Ice cubes
- Fresh mint leaves for garnish (optional)
- Peach slices for garnish (optional)

Instructions:

In a saucepan, bring 4 cups of water to a boil.

Add the tea bags to the boiling water and let it steep for 5-7 minutes, depending on your desired strength.

Remove the tea bags and stir in the sugar while the tea is still hot. Adjust the sweetness according to your taste preference.

Allow the sweetened tea to cool to room temperature.

In a blender, puree the sliced peaches until smooth.

Strain the peach puree through a fine-mesh sieve to remove any pulp, extracting the peach juice.

Combine the peach juice with the cooled sweetened tea.

Chill the peach iced tea in the refrigerator for at least 1-2 hours.

Fill glasses with ice cubes and pour the chilled peach iced tea over the ice.

Garnish with fresh mint leaves and peach slices if desired.

Stir gently before sipping to ensure the flavors are well mixed.

Enjoy your refreshing Peach Iced Tea!

Feel free to adjust the recipe to suit your taste. If you prefer a stronger tea flavor, you can steep the tea bags for a longer time. You can also experiment with using different types of black tea or adding a splash of lemon juice for extra brightness.

Lemon Lavender Iced Tea

Ingredients:

- 4-6 black tea bags
- 4 cups water
- 1/2 cup fresh lemon juice (about 3-4 lemons)
- Zest of 1 lemon
- 1/4 cup dried culinary lavender (or 2-3 tablespoons if using fresh lavender)
- 1/2 cup sugar (adjust to taste)
- Ice cubes
- Lemon slices for garnish (optional)
- Fresh lavender sprigs for garnish (optional)

Instructions:

In a saucepan, bring 4 cups of water to a boil.

Add the black tea bags and dried lavender to the boiling water. Let it steep for about 5-7 minutes, depending on your desired strength.

Remove the tea bags and strain out the lavender.

While the tea is still hot, stir in the sugar until it's fully dissolved.

Allow the sweetened lavender-infused tea to cool to room temperature.

Once cooled, add the fresh lemon juice and lemon zest to the tea. Stir to combine.

Chill the lemon lavender iced tea in the refrigerator for at least 1-2 hours.

Fill glasses with ice cubes and pour the chilled lemon lavender iced tea over the ice.

Garnish with lemon slices and fresh lavender sprigs if desired.

Stir gently before sipping to ensure the flavors are well mixed.

Enjoy your aromatic Lemon Lavender Iced Tea!

Feel free to adjust the sweetness and strength of the lavender flavor to your liking. If using fresh lavender, you can experiment with the quantity to find the right balance. This tea is perfect for a relaxing afternoon or as a unique and refreshing beverage for special occasions.

Raspberry Hibiscus Iced Tea

Ingredients:

- 4 cups water
- 4-6 hibiscus tea bags
- 1 cup fresh or frozen raspberries
- 1/2 cup sugar (adjust to taste)
- Ice cubes
- Fresh raspberries and mint leaves for garnish (optional)
- Lemon slices for garnish (optional)

Instructions:

In a saucepan, bring 4 cups of water to a boil.

Add the hibiscus tea bags to the boiling water and let it steep for about 5-7 minutes.

Remove the tea bags and stir in the sugar until it's fully dissolved. Adjust the sweetness according to your taste preference.

Allow the hibiscus tea to cool to room temperature.

In a blender, puree the raspberries until smooth.

Strain the raspberry puree through a fine-mesh sieve to remove the seeds, extracting the raspberry juice.

Combine the raspberry juice with the cooled hibiscus tea.

Chill the raspberry hibiscus iced tea in the refrigerator for at least 1-2 hours.

Fill glasses with ice cubes and pour the chilled raspberry hibiscus iced tea over the ice.

Garnish with fresh raspberries, mint leaves, and lemon slices if desired.

Stir gently before sipping to ensure the flavors are well mixed.

Enjoy your refreshing Raspberry Hibiscus Iced Tea!

Feel free to customize the recipe based on your preferences. If you like a stronger tea flavor, you can steep the hibiscus tea bags for a longer time. Experiment with the sweetness and the ratio of raspberry juice to hibiscus tea to suit your taste. This iced tea is perfect for warm days and a lovely way to enjoy the flavors of raspberry and hibiscus.

Minty Mango Iced Tea

Ingredients:

- 4 cups water
- 4-6 black tea bags
- 1 ripe mango, peeled, pitted, and diced
- 1/4 cup fresh mint leaves
- 1/2 cup sugar (adjust to taste)
- Ice cubes
- Fresh mango slices and mint sprigs for garnish (optional)
- Lemon slices for garnish (optional)

Instructions:

In a saucepan, bring 4 cups of water to a boil.

Add the black tea bags to the boiling water and let it steep for about 5-7 minutes.

Remove the tea bags and stir in the sugar until it's fully dissolved. Adjust the sweetness according to your taste preference.

Allow the sweetened tea to cool to room temperature.

In a blender, puree the diced mango and fresh mint leaves until smooth.

Strain the mango-mint puree through a fine-mesh sieve to remove any pulp, extracting the mango-mint juice.

Combine the mango-mint juice with the cooled sweetened tea.

Chill the Minty Mango Iced Tea in the refrigerator for at least 1-2 hours.

Fill glasses with ice cubes and pour the chilled Minty Mango Iced Tea over the ice.

Garnish with fresh mango slices, mint sprigs, and lemon slices if desired.

Stir gently before sipping to ensure the flavors are well mixed.

Enjoy your tropical and minty Minty Mango Iced Tea!

Feel free to customize the recipe based on your preferences. If you prefer a stronger tea flavor, you can steep the tea bags for a longer time. Experiment with the sweetness and the ratio of mango-mint juice to tea to suit your taste. This iced tea is perfect for cooling down on a hot day with the delightful combination of mango and mint.

Orange Blossom Iced Tea

Ingredients:

- 4 cups water
- 4-6 black tea bags
- 1/4 cup sugar (adjust to taste)
- 1/4 cup fresh orange juice
- 1 teaspoon orange zest
- 1-2 tablespoons orange blossom water (adjust to taste)
- Ice cubes
- Orange slices for garnish (optional)
- Fresh mint leaves for garnish (optional)

Instructions:

In a saucepan, bring 4 cups of water to a boil.

Add the black tea bags to the boiling water and let it steep for about 5-7 minutes.

Remove the tea bags and stir in the sugar until it's fully dissolved. Adjust the sweetness according to your taste preference.

Allow the sweetened tea to cool to room temperature.

Add fresh orange juice, orange zest, and orange blossom water to the cooled sweetened tea. Stir to combine.

Chill the Orange Blossom Iced Tea in the refrigerator for at least 1-2 hours.

Fill glasses with ice cubes and pour the chilled Orange Blossom Iced Tea over the ice.

Garnish with orange slices and fresh mint leaves if desired.

Stir gently before sipping to ensure the flavors are well mixed.

Enjoy your refreshing Orange Blossom Iced Tea!

Feel free to customize the recipe based on your preferences. If you enjoy a stronger citrus flavor, you can add more orange juice or zest. Adjust the amount of orange blossom water to achieve your desired level of floral aroma. This iced tea is a delightful and aromatic drink for warm days.

Ginger Peach Iced Tea

Ingredients:

- 4 cups water
- 4-6 black tea bags
- 2 ripe peaches, pitted and sliced
- 1-2 tablespoons fresh ginger, peeled and sliced
- 1/4 cup sugar (adjust to taste)
- Ice cubes
- Peach slices and fresh mint leaves for garnish (optional)

Instructions:

In a saucepan, bring 4 cups of water to a boil.

Add the black tea bags to the boiling water and let it steep for about 5-7 minutes.

Remove the tea bags and stir in the sugar until it's fully dissolved. Adjust the sweetness according to your taste preference.

While the tea is still hot, add the sliced peaches and fresh ginger to the pot.

Allow the ginger and peaches to steep in the tea until it reaches room temperature.

Strain the tea to remove the peach slices and ginger pieces.

Chill the Ginger Peach Iced Tea in the refrigerator for at least 1-2 hours.

Fill glasses with ice cubes and pour the chilled Ginger Peach Iced Tea over the ice.

Garnish with peach slices and fresh mint leaves if desired.

Stir gently before sipping to ensure the flavors are well mixed.

Enjoy your refreshing Ginger Peach Iced Tea!

Feel free to customize the recipe based on your preferences. If you prefer a stronger ginger flavor, you can adjust the amount of fresh ginger slices. You can also experiment with adding a splash of lemon juice for extra brightness. This iced tea is perfect for cooling down on a hot day with the delightful combination of ginger and peach flavors.

Berry Burst Iced Tea

Ingredients:

- 4 cups water
- 4-6 black tea bags
- 1 cup mixed berries (such as strawberries, blueberries, raspberries, and blackberries)
- 1/4 cup sugar (adjust to taste)
- Ice cubes
- Mixed berries for garnish (optional)
- Fresh mint leaves for garnish (optional)

Instructions:

In a saucepan, bring 4 cups of water to a boil.

Add the black tea bags to the boiling water and let it steep for about 5-7 minutes.

Remove the tea bags and stir in the sugar until it's fully dissolved. Adjust the sweetness according to your taste preference.

Allow the sweetened tea to cool to room temperature.

In a blender, puree the mixed berries until smooth.

Strain the berry puree through a fine-mesh sieve to remove seeds and pulp, extracting the berry juice.

Combine the berry juice with the cooled sweetened tea.

Chill the Berry Burst Iced Tea in the refrigerator for at least 1-2 hours.

Fill glasses with ice cubes and pour the chilled Berry Burst Iced Tea over the ice.

Garnish with additional mixed berries and fresh mint leaves if desired.

Stir gently before sipping to ensure the flavors are well mixed.

Enjoy your refreshing Berry Burst Iced Tea!

Feel free to customize the recipe based on your preferences. You can use your favorite combination of berries, and if you prefer a stronger tea flavor, you can steep the tea bags for a longer time. This iced tea is a delightful way to enjoy the natural sweetness and vibrant colors of assorted berries.

Cranberry Apple Iced Tea

Ingredients:

- 4 cups water
- 4-6 black tea bags
- 1 cup cranberry juice (100% pure, unsweetened)
- 1 cup apple juice (100% pure, unsweetened)
- 1/4 cup sugar (adjust to taste)
- Ice cubes
- Apple slices and fresh cranberries for garnish (optional)
- Fresh mint leaves for garnish (optional)

Instructions:

In a saucepan, bring 4 cups of water to a boil.

Add the black tea bags to the boiling water and let it steep for about 5-7 minutes.

Remove the tea bags and stir in the sugar until it's fully dissolved. Adjust the sweetness according to your taste preference.

Allow the sweetened tea to cool to room temperature.

In a separate container, mix together the cranberry juice and apple juice.

Combine the mixed juices with the cooled sweetened tea.

Chill the Cranberry Apple Iced Tea in the refrigerator for at least 1-2 hours.

Fill glasses with ice cubes and pour the chilled Cranberry Apple Iced Tea over the ice.

Garnish with apple slices, fresh cranberries, and mint leaves if desired.

Stir gently before sipping to ensure the flavors are well mixed.

Enjoy your delightful Cranberry Apple Iced Tea!

Feel free to customize the recipe based on your preferences. If you prefer a stronger tea flavor, you can steep the tea bags for a longer time. Adjust the sweetness and the ratio of cranberry juice to apple juice to suit your taste. This iced tea is a wonderful blend of fru ty goodness and the classic appeal of iced tea.

Blueberry Mint Iced Tea

Ingredients:

- 4 cups water
- 4-6 black tea bags
- 1 cup fresh or frozen blueberries
- 1/4 cup fresh mint leaves
- 1/4 cup sugar (adjust to taste)
- Ice cubes
- Fresh blueberries and mint sprigs for garnish (optional)
- Lemon slices for garnish (optional)

Instructions:

In a saucepan, bring 4 cups of water to a boil.

Add the black tea bags to the boiling water and let it steep for about 5-7 minutes.

Remove the tea bags and stir in the sugar until it's fully dissolved. Adjust the sweetness according to your taste preference.

Allow the sweetened tea to cool to room temperature.

In a blender, combine the blueberries and fresh mint leaves. Blend until you get a smooth puree.

Strain the blueberry-mint puree through a fine-mesh sieve to remove any solids, extracting the juice.

Combine the blueberry-mint juice with the cooled sweetened tea.

Chill the Blueberry Mint Iced Tea in the refrigerator for at least 1-2 hours.

Fill glasses with ice cubes and pour the chilled Blueberry Mint Iced Tea over the ice.

Garnish with fresh blueberries and mint sprigs. Add lemon slices if desired.

Stir gently before sipping to ensure the flavors are well mixed.

Enjoy your refreshing Blueberry Mint Iced Tea!

Feel free to customize the recipe based on your preferences. If you prefer a stronger tea flavor, you can steep the tea bags for a longer time. Adjust the sweetness and the ratio of blueberry-mint juice to tea to suit your taste. This iced tea is a delightful way to enjoy the combination of blueberries and mint on a warm day.

Chamomile Citrus Iced Tea

Ingredients:

- 4 cups water
- 4-6 chamomile tea bags
- 1 orange, sliced
- 1 lemon, sliced
- 1/4 cup honey (adjust to taste)
- Ice cubes
- Fresh chamomile flowers, orange slices, and lemon slices for garnish (optional)
- Fresh mint leaves for garnish (optional)

Instructions:

In a saucepan, bring 4 cups of water to a boil.

Add the chamomile tea bags to the boiling water and let it steep for about 5-7 minutes.

Remove the tea bags and stir in the honey until it's fully dissolved. Adjust the sweetness according to your taste preference.

Allow the sweetened chamomile tea to cool to room temperature.

In a pitcher, combine the cooled chamomile tea with slices of orange and lemon.

Chill the Chamomile Citrus Iced Tea in the refrigerator for at least 1-2 hours.

Fill glasses with ice cubes and pour the chilled Chamomile Citrus Iced Tea over the ice.

Garnish with fresh chamomile flowers, orange slices, lemon slices, and mint leaves if desired.

Stir gently before sipping to ensure the flavors are well mixed.

Enjoy your calming and citrusy Chamomile Citrus Iced Tea!

Feel free to customize the recipe based on your preferences. You can add more honey if you prefer a sweeter tea or adjust the quantity of citrus slices for a stronger citrus flavor. This iced tea is perfect for relaxation and enjoyment on a sunny day.

Lemonades

Classic Lemonade

Ingredients:

- 1 cup fresh lemon juice (about 4-6 lemons)
- 1 cup granulated sugar
- 4 cups cold water
- Ice cubes
- Lemon slices for garnish (optional)
- Fresh mint leaves for garnish (optional)

Instructions:

In a small saucepan, combine 1 cup of water and the granulated sugar. Heat over medium heat, stirring occasionally, until the sugar completely dissolves. This creates a simple syrup. Allow it to cool.

While the simple syrup is cooling, juice the lemons to obtain 1 cup of fresh lemon juice.

In a pitcher, combine the fresh lemon juice and the cooled simple syrup.

Add 4 cups of cold water to the pitcher and stir well to mix the lemon juice, simple syrup, and water.

Taste the lemonade and adjust the sweetness by adding more sugar or water if needed.

Refrigerate the lemonade for at least 1-2 hours to chill.

When ready to serve, fill glasses with ice cubes and pour the chilled Classic Lemonade over the ice.

Garnish with lemon slices and fresh mint leaves if desired.

Stir gently before sipping to ensure the flavors are well mixed.

Enjoy your refreshing Classic Lemonade!

Feel free to customize the recipe based on your preferences. If you like a stronger lemon flavor, you can add more lemon juice. Adjust the sweetness to your taste by varying the amount of sugar in the simple syrup. This classic lemonade is perfect for quenching your thirst on a hot day.

Strawberry Lemonade

Ingredients:

- 1 cup fresh lemon juice (about 4-6 lemons)
- 1 cup fresh strawberries, hulled and halved
- 1 cup granulated sugar
- 4 cups cold water
- Ice cubes
- Lemon slices and whole strawberries for garnish (optional)
- Fresh mint leaves for garnish (optional)

Instructions:

In a blender, combine the fresh lemon juice, fresh strawberries, and granulated sugar. Blend until the strawberries are fully pureed.

Strain the strawberry-lemon mixture through a fine-mesh sieve into a pitcher to remove seeds and pulp, extracting the juice.

In the pitcher, add 4 cups of cold water to the strawberry-lemon juice. Stir well to combine.

Taste the strawberry lemonade and adjust the sweetness by adding more sugar if needed.

Refrigerate the strawberry lemonade for at least 1-2 hours to chill.

When ready to serve, fill glasses with ice cubes and pour the chilled Strawberry Lemonade over the ice.

Garnish with lemon slices, whole strawberries, and fresh mint leaves if desired.

Stir gently before sipping to ensure the flavors are well mixed.

Enjoy your delightful Strawberry Lemonade!

Feel free to customize the recipe based on your preferences. You can adjust the sweetness, add more strawberries for a stronger berry flavor, or even muddle some fresh mint into the mixture for an extra element of freshness. Strawberry Lemonade is a perfect way to enjoy the sweetness of strawberries with the tartness of lemons.

Lavender Lemonade

Ingredients:

- 1 cup fresh lemon juice (about 4-6 lemons)
- 1 tablespoon dried culinary lavender (or 2-3 tablespoons if using fresh lavender)
- 1 cup granulated sugar
- 4 cups water
- Ice cubes
- Lemon slices and fresh lavender sprigs for garnish (optional)

Instructions:

In a small saucepan, combine 1 cup of water and the granulated sugar. Heat over medium heat, stirring occasionally, until the sugar completely dissolves. This creates a simple syrup.

Remove the saucepan from heat and add the dried lavender to the simple syrup. Let it steep for about 15-20 minutes. If using fresh lavender, steep for a shorter time, about 5-10 minutes.

Strain the lavender-infused simple syrup through a fine-mesh sieve into a pitcher to remove the lavender buds, extracting the lavender-flavored syrup.

In the pitcher, combine the fresh lemon juice with the lavender-infused simple syrup.

Add 4 cups of cold water to the pitcher and stir well to mix the lemon juice, lavender syrup, and water.

Taste the lavender lemonade and adjust the sweetness by adding more sugar or water if needed.

Refrigerate the lavender lemonade for at least 1-2 hours to chill.

When ready to serve, fill glasses with ice cubes and pour the chilled Lavender Lemonade over the ice.

Garnish with lemon slices and fresh lavender sprigs if desired.

Stir gently before sipping to ensure the flavors are well mixed.

Enjoy your calming and aromatic Lavender Lemonade!

Feel free to customize the recipe based on your preferences. If you enjoy a stronger lavender flavor, you can steep the lavender for a longer time. Lavender Lemonade is a lovely and refreshing drink, perfect for a relaxing afternoon.

Basil Blueberry Lemonade

Ingredients:

- 1 cup fresh blueberries
- 1 cup fresh lemon juice (about 4-6 lemons)
- 1 cup granulated sugar
- 1 bunch fresh basil leaves (about 1 cup loosely packed)
- 4 cups water
- Ice cubes
- Lemon slices, blueberries, and basil leaves for garnish (optional)

Instructions:

In a blender, combine the fresh blueberries, fresh lemon juice, and granulated sugar. Blend until the blueberries are fully pureed.

In a saucepan, combine 1 cup of water with the basil leaves. Heat over medium heat until it reaches a simmer. Simmer for about 5 minutes to infuse the basil flavor into the water.

Strain the basil-infused water through a fine-mesh sieve into a pitcher, extracting the basil-flavored liquid.

In the pitcher, combine the blueberry-lemon puree with the basil-infused water. Add 3 more cups of cold water to the pitcher and stir well to mix the blueberry-lemon-basil mixture with water.

Taste the basil blueberry lemonade and adjust the sweetness by adding more sugar or water if needed.

Refrigerate the basil blueberry lemonade for at least 1-2 hours to chill.

When ready to serve, fill glasses with ice cubes and pour the chilled Basil Blueberry Lemonade over the ice.

Garnish with lemon slices, fresh blueberries, and basil leaves if desired.

Stir gently before sipping to ensure the flavors are well mixed.

Enjoy your delightful Basil Blueberry Lemonade!

Feel free to customize the recipe based on your preferences. If you enjoy a stronger basil flavor, you can infuse the water for a longer time. This unique twist on lemonade is perfect for a refreshing and herb-infused beverage.

Pineapple GInger Lemonade

Ingredients:

- 1 cup fresh pineapple juice
- 1 cup fresh lemon juice (about 4-6 lemons)
- 1/4 cup fresh ginger, peeled and grated
- 1 cup granulated sugar
- 4 cups water
- Ice cubes
- Pineapple slices, lemon slices, and ginger slices for garnish (optional)
- Fresh mint leaves for garnish (optional)

Instructions:

In a small saucepan, combine 1 cup of water with the grated ginger. Heat over medium heat until it reaches a simmer. Simmer for about 5 minutes to infuse the ginger flavor into the water.

Strain the ginger-infused water through a fine-mesh sieve into a pitcher, extracting the ginger-flavored liquid.

In the pitcher, combine the fresh pineapple juice, fresh lemon juice, and granulated sugar.

Add the ginger-infused water to the pitcher and stir well to mix the pineapple-lemon-ginger combination with water.

Taste the pineapple ginger lemonade and adjust the sweetness by adding more sugar or water if needed.

Refrigerate the pineapple ginger lemonade for at least 1-2 hours to chill.

When ready to serve, fill glasses with ice cubes and pour the chilled Pineapple Ginger Lemonade over the ice.

Garnish with pineapple slices, lemon slices, and ginger slices if desired. Add fresh mint leaves for an extra burst of flavor.

Stir gently before sipping to ensure the flavors are well mixed.

Enjoy your tropical and zesty Pineapple Ginger Lemonade!

Feel free to customize the recipe based on your preferences. If you enjoy a stronger ginger flavor, you can infuse the water for a longer time or add more grated ginger. This refreshing lemonade is perfect for a summer day or any time you're craving a tropical twist.

Raspberry Mint Lemonade

Ingredients:

- 1 cup fresh raspberries
- 1 cup fresh lemon juice (about 4-6 lemons)
- 1 cup granulated sugar
- 1 bunch fresh mint leaves (about 1 cup loosely packed)
- 4 cups water
- Ice cubes
- Fresh raspberries, lemon slices, and mint sprigs for garnish (optional)

Instructions:

In a blender, combine the fresh raspberries, fresh lemon juice, and granulated sugar. Blend until the raspberries are fully pureed.

In a saucepan, combine 1 cup of water with the mint leaves. Heat over medium heat until it reaches a simmer. Simmer for about 5 minutes to infuse the mint flavor into the water.

Strain the mint-infused water through a fine-mesh sieve into a pitcher, extracting the mint-flavored liquid.

In the pitcher, combine the raspberry-lemon puree with the mint-infused water. Add 3 more cups of cold water to the pitcher and stir well to mix the raspberry-lemon-mint combination with water.

Taste the raspberry mint lemonade and adjust the sweetness by adding more sugar or water if needed.

Refrigerate the raspberry mint lemonade for at least 1-2 hours to chill.

When ready to serve, fill glasses with ice cubes and pour the chilled Raspberry Mint Lemonade over the ice.

Garnish with fresh raspberries, lemon slices, and mint sprigs if desired.

Stir gently before sipping to ensure the flavors are well mixed.

Enjoy your refreshing Raspberry Mint Lemonade!

Feel free to customize the recipe based on your preferences. If you enjoy a stronger mint flavor, you can infuse the water for a longer time. This vibrant and fruity lemonade is perfect for cooling down on a warm day.

Cucumber Rosemary Lemonade

Ingredients:

- 1 cucumber, thinly sliced
- 1 cup fresh lemon juice (about 4-6 lemons)
- 1 cup granulated sugar
- 1 sprig fresh rosemary
- 4 cups water
- Ice cubes
- Cucumber slices, lemon slices, and rosemary sprigs for garnish (optional)

Instructions:

In a saucepan, combine 1 cup of water with the granulated sugar. Heat over medium heat, stirring occasionally, until the sugar completely dissolves. This creates a simple syrup.

Add the sprig of fresh rosemary to the simple syrup. Let it steep for about 10-15 minutes to infuse the rosemary flavor into the syrup.

Strain the rosemary-infused simple syrup through a fine-mesh sieve into a pitcher, extracting the rosemary-flavored liquid.

In the pitcher, combine the fresh cucumber slices with the rosemary-infused simple syrup.

Add the fresh lemon juice to the pitcher and stir well to mix the cucumber-rosemary-lemon combination with water.

Add 3 more cups of cold water to the pitcher and stir again.

Taste the cucumber rosemary lemonade and adjust the sweetness by adding more sugar or water if needed.

Refrigerate the cucumber rosemary lemonade for at least 1-2 hours to chill.

When ready to serve, fill glasses with ice cubes and pour the chilled Cucumber Rosemary Lemonade over the ice.

Garnish with cucumber slices, lemon slices, and rosemary sprigs if desired.

Stir gently before sipping to ensure the flavors are well mixed.

Enjoy your uniquely flavored Cucumber Rosemary Lemonade!

Feel free to customize the recipe based on your preferences. If you enjoy a stronger rosemary flavor, you can steep the herb for a longer time. This cucumber rosemary lemonade is a perfect choice for a sophisticated and refreshing drink.

Watermelon Basil Lemonade

Ingredients:

- 4 cups cubed seedless watermelon
- 1 cup fresh lemon juice (about 4-6 lemons)
- 1 cup granulated sugar
- 1 bunch fresh basil leaves (about 1 cup loosely packed)
- 4 cups water
- Ice cubes
- Watermelon slices, lemon slices, and basil leaves for garnish (optional)

Instructions:

In a blender, puree the cubed watermelon until smooth.

In a small saucepan, combine 1 cup of water with the granulated sugar. Heat over medium heat, stirring occasionally, until the sugar completely dissolves. This creates a simple syrup.

In the pitcher, combine the fresh watermelon puree with the fresh lemon juice.

Add the fresh basil leaves to the simple syrup and let it steep for about 10-15 minutes to infuse the basil flavor into the syrup.

Strain the basil-infused simple syrup through a fine-mesh sieve into the pitcher, extracting the basil-flavored liquid.

Add 3 more cups of cold water to the pitcher and stir well to mix the watermelon-lemon-basil combination with water.

Taste the watermelon basil lemonade and adjust the sweetness by adding more sugar or water if needed.

Refrigerate the watermelon basil lemonade for at least 1-2 hours to chill.

When ready to serve, fill glasses with ice cubes and pour the chilled Watermelon Basil Lemonade over the ice.

Garnish with watermelon slices, lemon slices, and fresh basil leaves if desired.

Stir gently before sipping to ensure the flavors are well mixed.

Enjoy your refreshing Watermelon Basil Lemonade!

Feel free to customize the recipe based on your preferences. If you enjoy a stronger basil flavor, you can steep the herb for a longer time. This watermelon basil lemonade is a perfect choice for staying cool and refreshed on a hot day.

Mango Tango Lemonade

Ingredients:

- 1 cup fresh mango puree (from ripe mangoes)
- 1 cup fresh lemon juice (about 4-6 lemons)
- 1 cup granulated sugar
- 4 cups water
- Ice cubes
- Mango slices and lemon slices for garnish (optional)
- Fresh mint leaves for garnish (optional)

Instructions:

In a blender, puree ripe mangoes until smooth to obtain 1 cup of fresh mango puree.

In a small saucepan, combine 1 cup of water with the granulated sugar. Heat over medium heat, stirring occasionally, until the sugar completely dissolves. This creates a simple syrup.

In the pitcher, combine the fresh mango puree with the fresh lemon juice.

Add the simple syrup to the mango-lemon mixture and stir well to combine.

Add 3 more cups of cold water to the pitcher and stir again.

Taste the mango tango lemonade and adjust the sweetness by adding more sugar or water if needed.

Refrigerate the mango tango lemonade for at least 1-2 hours to chill.

When ready to serve, fill glasses with ice cubes and pour the chilled Mango Tango Lemonade over the ice.

Garnish with mango slices, lemon slices, and fresh mint leaves if desired.

Stir gently before sipping to ensure the flavors are well mixed.

Enjoy your tropical and fruity Mango Tango Lemonade!

Feel free to customize the recipe based on your preferences. If you like a stronger mango flavor, you can add more mango puree. This vibrant and exotic lemonade is perfect for enjoying the tropical goodness of mango on a sunny day.

Infused Waters

Cucumber Mint Infused Water

Ingredients:

- 1/2 cucumber, thinly sliced
- 1/4 cup fresh mint leaves
- 1-2 liters of water (depending on your preference for strength)

Instructions:

Wash the cucumber thoroughly and slice it thinly.

Rinse the fresh mint leaves.

In a large pitcher, combine the cucumber slices and mint leaves.

Fill the pitcher with 1-2 liters of water, depending on how strong you'd like the infusion.

Refrigerate the cucumber mint infused water for at least 1-2 hours to allow the flavors to meld.

If you prefer a stronger flavor, you can let the water infuse for a longer period.

Before serving, you can strain the cucumber and mint from the water if desired, or leave them in for visual appeal.

Pour the infused water into glasses filled with ice cubes.

Garnish with additional cucumber slices and mint leaves if desired.

Stir gently before sipping to ensure the flavors are well mixed.

Enjoy your cool and revitalizing Cucumber Mint Infused Water!

This infused water is a great way to stay hydrated with the subtle flavors of cucumber and mint. It's a healthy and refreshing alternative to plain water, making it perfect for hot days or as a spa-like beverage.

Strawberry Basil Infused Water

Ingredients:

- 1 cup fresh strawberries, hulled and halved
- 1/4 cup fresh basil leaves
- 1-2 liters of water (depending on your preference for strength)

Instructions:

Wash the strawberries and basil leaves thoroughly.

Hull the strawberries and cut them in half.

In a large pitcher, combine the fresh strawberries and basil leaves.

Fill the pitcher with 1-2 liters of water, depending on how strong you'd like the infusion.

Refrigerate the strawberry basil infused water for at least 1-2 hours to allow the flavors to meld.

If you prefer a stronger flavor, you can let the water infuse for a longer period.

Before serving, you can strain the strawberries and basil from the water if desired, or leave them in for visual appeal.

Pour the infused water into glasses filled with ice cubes.

Garnish with additional strawberry slices and basil leaves if desired.

Stir gently before sipping to ensure the flavors are well mixed.

Enjoy your delicious Strawberry Basil Infused Water!

This infused water not only adds a burst of fruity and herbal flavor but also makes staying hydrated more enjoyable. It's a perfect beverage for warm days, and you can experiment with the ratio of strawberries to basil to find your ideal balance of flavors.

Citrus Rosemary Infused Water

Ingredients:

- 1 orange, thinly sliced
- 1 lemon, thinly sliced
- 1 lime, thinly sliced
- 1 sprig fresh rosemary
- 1-2 liters of water (depending on your preference for strength)

Instructions:

Wash the citrus fruits thoroughly.

Thinly slice the orange, lemon, and lime.

In a large pitcher, combine the sliced citrus fruits and the fresh rosemary sprig.

Fill the pitcher with 1-2 liters of water, depending on how strong you'd like the infusion.

Gently muddle the ingredients in the pitcher to release the flavors of the citrus and rosemary.

Refrigerate the citrus rosemary infused water for at least 1-2 hours to allow the flavors to meld.

If you prefer a stronger flavor, you can let the water infuse for a longer period.

Before serving, you can remove the sliced citrus and rosemary or leave them in for visual appeal.

Pour the infused water into glasses filled with ice cubes.

Garnish with additional citrus slices and a fresh rosemary sprig if desired.

Stir gently before sipping to ensure the flavors are well mixed.

Enjoy your revitalizing Citrus Rosemary Infused Water!

This infused water offers a zesty and herbal combination, making it a perfect choice for a refreshing drink. Experiment with the citrus fruits and rosemary to find the balance of flavors that suits your taste.

Blueberry Lavender Infused Water

Ingredients:

- 1 cup fresh blueberries
- 1-2 tablespoons dried culinary lavender (adjust to taste)
- 1-2 liters of water (depending on your preference for strength)

Instructions:

Wash the fresh blueberries thoroughly.

In a large pitcher, combine the fresh blueberries with the dried culinary lavender.

Fill the pitcher with 1-2 liters of water, depending on how strong you'd like the infusion.

Gently muddle the blueberries and lavender in the pitcher to release their flavors.

Refrigerate the blueberry lavender infused water for at least 1-2 hours to allow the flavors to meld.

If you prefer a stronger flavor, you can let the water infuse for a longer period.

Before serving, you can strain the blueberries and lavender or leave them in for visual appeal.

Pour the infused water into glasses filled with ice cubes.

Garnish with additional blueberries and a sprig of lavender if desired.

Stir gently before sipping to ensure the flavors are well mixed.

Enjoy your flavorful and fragrant Blueberry Lavender Infused Water!

This infused water offers a unique blend of fruity sweetness and floral notes. Adjust the amount of lavender to suit your taste preference. It's a refreshing drink that's perfect for staying hydrated in a delightful way.

Pineapple Coconut Infused Water

Ingredients:

- 1 cup fresh pineapple chunks
- 1/2 cup coconut chunks or coconut water
- 1-2 liters of water (depending on your preference for strength)

Instructions:

Peel and chop fresh pineapple into chunks.

If using coconut chunks, crack open a fresh coconut and cut the flesh into smaller pieces. Alternatively, you can use coconut water for a lighter coconut flavor.

In a large pitcher, combine the fresh pineapple chunks with the coconut chunks or coconut water.

Fill the pitcher with 1-2 liters of water, depending on how strong you'd like the infusion.

Gently muddle the pineapple and coconut in the pitcher to release their flavors.

Refrigerate the pineapple coconut infused water for at least 1-2 hours to allow the flavors to meld.

If you prefer a stronger flavor, you can let the water infuse for a longer period.

Before serving, you can strain out the pineapple and coconut pieces or leave them in for visual appeal.

Pour the infused water into glasses filled with ice cubes.

Garnish with additional pineapple chunks or coconut slices if desired.

Stir gently before sipping to ensure the flavors are well mixed.

Enjoy your tropical Pineapple Coconut Infused Water!

Feel free to customize the recipe based on your preferences. This infused water provides a taste of the tropics and is a perfect way to stay hydrated with a hint of natural sweetness.

Watermelon Mint Infused Water

Ingredients:

- 2 cups seedless watermelon, cut into small cubes
- 1/4 cup fresh mint leaves
- 1-2 liters of water (depending on your preference for strength)

Instructions:

Cut the seedless watermelon into small cubes.

Wash the fresh mint leaves thoroughly.

In a large pitcher, combine the watermelon cubes with the fresh mint leaves.

Fill the pitcher with 1-2 liters of water, depending on how strong you'd like the infusion.

Gently muddle the watermelon and mint in the pitcher to release their flavors.

Refrigerate the watermelon mint infused water for at least 1-2 hours to allow the flavors to meld.

If you prefer a stronger flavor, you can let the water infuse for a longer period.

Before serving, you can strain out the watermelon and mint or leave them in for visual appeal.

Pour the infused water into glasses filled with ice cubes.

Garnish with additional watermelon cubes or mint leaves if desired.

Stir gently before sipping to ensure the flavors are well mixed.

Enjoy your refreshing Watermelon Mint Infused Water!

Feel free to customize the recipe based on your preferences. This infused water is a delicious way to enjoy the natural sweetness of watermelon with a hint of mint. It's perfect for staying cool and hydrated on a hot day.

Kiwi Cucumber Infused Water

Ingredients:

- 2 kiwis, peeled and sliced
- 1/2 cucumber, thinly sliced
- 1-2 liters of water (depending on your preference for strength)

Instructions:

Peel and slice the kiwis.

Wash the cucumber thoroughly and slice it thinly.

In a large pitcher, combine the sliced kiwis with the sliced cucumber.

Fill the pitcher with 1-2 liters of water, depending on how strong you'd like the infusion.

Gently muddle the kiwi and cucumber in the pitcher to release their flavors.

Refrigerate the kiwi cucumber infused water for at least 1-2 hours to allow the flavors to meld.

If you prefer a stronger flavor, you can let the water infuse for a longer period.

Before serving, you can strain out the kiwi and cucumber slices or leave them in for visual appeal.

Pour the infused water into glasses filled with ice cubes.

Garnish with additional kiwi slices or cucumber slices if desired.

Stir gently before sipping to ensure the flavors are well mixed.

Enjoy your tropical Kiwi Cucumber Infused Water!

Feel free to customize the recipe based on your preferences. This infused water offers a delightful combination of tropical sweetness and refreshing cucumber. It's a great way to stay hydrated with a burst of natural flavor.

Mango Pineapple Infused Water

Ingredients:

- 1 cup fresh mango chunks
- 1 cup fresh pineapple chunks
- 1-2 liters of water (depending on your preference for strength)

Instructions:

Peel and cut the fresh mango into chunks.

Cut the fresh pineapple into chunks.

In a large pitcher, combine the mango chunks with the pineapple chunks.

Fill the pitcher with 1-2 liters of water, depending on how strong you'd like the infusion.

Gently muddle the mango and pineapple in the pitcher to release their flavors.

Refrigerate the mango pineapple infused water for at least 1-2 hours to allow the flavors to meld.

If you prefer a stronger flavor, you can let the water infuse for a longer period.

Before serving, you can strain out the mango and pineapple chunks or leave them in for visual appeal.

Pour the infused water into glasses filled with ice cubes.

Garnish with additional mango or pineapple chunks if desired.

Stir gently before sipping to ensure the flavors are well mixed.

Enjoy your tropical Mango Pineapple Infused Water!

Feel free to customize the recipe based on your preferences. This infused water provides a taste of the tropics and is a perfect way to stay hydrated with a hint of natural sweetness.

Raspberry Lime Infused Water

Ingredients:

- 1 cup fresh raspberries
- 2 limes, thinly sliced
- 1-2 liters of water (depending on your preference for strength)

Instructions:

Wash the fresh raspberries and limes thoroughly.

In a large pitcher, combine the fresh raspberries with the thinly sliced limes.

Fill the pitcher with 1-2 liters of water, depending on how strong you'd like the infusion.

Gently muddle the raspberries and lime slices in the pitcher to release their flavors.

Refrigerate the raspberry lime infused water for at least 1-2 hours to allow the flavors to meld.

If you prefer a stronger flavor, you can let the water infuse for a longer period.

Before serving, you can strain out the raspberries and lime slices or leave them in for visual appeal.

Pour the infused water into glasses filled with ice cubes.

Garnish with additional raspberries and lime slices if desired.

Stir gently before sipping to ensure the flavors are well mixed.

Enjoy your refreshing Raspberry Lime Infused Water!

Feel free to customize the recipe based on your preferences. This infused water provides a delightful blend of berry sweetness and citrusy tang, making it a perfect choice for staying hydrated with a burst of natural flavor.

Orange Ginger Infused Water

Ingredients:

- 2 oranges, thinly sliced
- 1-2 inches fresh ginger, peeled and thinly sliced
- 1-2 liters of water (depending on your preference for strength)

Instructions:

Wash the oranges and ginger thoroughly.

Thinly slice the oranges.

Peel and thinly slice the fresh ginger.

In a large pitcher, combine the sliced oranges with the sliced ginger.

Fill the pitcher with 1-2 liters of water, depending on how strong you'd like the infusion.

Gently muddle the orange slices and ginger in the pitcher to release their flavors.

Refrigerate the orange ginger infused water for at least 1-2 hours to allow the flavors to meld.

If you prefer a stronger flavor, you can let the water infuse for a longer period.

Before serving, you can strain out the orange slices and ginger or leave them in for visual appeal.

Pour the infused water into glasses filled with ice cubes.

Garnish with additional orange slices or ginger slices if desired.

Stir gently before sipping to ensure the flavors are well mixed.

Enjoy your zesty Orange Ginger Infused Water!

Feel free to customize the recipe based on your preferences. This infused water provides a refreshing combination of citrus and spice, making it a fantastic choice for a flavorful and hydrating drink.

Hot Drinks

Apple Cinnamon Hot Toddy (Non-Alcoholic)

Ingredients:

- 1 cup apple juice or apple cider
- 1 cinnamon stick
- 1-2 cloves
- 1-2 slices of fresh ginger
- 1 tablespoon honey (adjust to taste)
- Lemon wedge (optional, for garnish)
- Cinnamon powder (optional, for garnish)

Instructions:

In a small saucepan, heat the apple juice or apple cider over medium heat until it's warm but not boiling.

Add the cinnamon stick, cloves, and fresh ginger slices to the saucepan. These ingredients will infuse the hot toddy with warm and comforting flavors.

Allow the mixture to simmer for about 5-7 minutes, allowing the spices to infuse into the apple juice.

Remove the saucepan from the heat and strain the mixture to remove the spices. You can use a fine-mesh sieve or simply remove the spices with a spoon.

Stir in honey to sweeten the hot toddy. Adjust the amount to your desired level of sweetness.

Pour the non-alcoholic hot toddy into a mug.

Optionally, garnish with a wedge of lemon and a sprinkle of cinnamon powder for added flavor and aroma.

Stir the hot toddy gently and let it cool slightly before sipping.

Enjoy your cozy and soothing Non-Alcoholic Apple Cinnamon Hot Toddy!

This beverage is perfect for warming up on a chilly day or as a comforting bedtime drink. Adjust the ingredients to suit your taste preferences, and feel free to experiment with additional spices like nutmeg or allspice for extra warmth.

Spiced Chai Latte

Ingredients:

- 2 cups water
- 2 black tea bags or 2 tablespoons loose black tea
- 1 cinnamon stick
- 4-6 whole cloves
- 4-6 cardamom pods, crushed
- 1-2 slices fresh ginger
- 2 cups milk (dairy or non-dairy)
- 2-4 tablespoons sweetener (sugar, honey, or maple syrup)
- Optional: whipped cream, ground cinnamon, or cinnamon sticks for garnish

Instructions:

In a saucepan, bring the water to a boil.

Add the black tea bags or loose black tea, cinnamon stick, cloves, crushed cardamom pods, and fresh ginger slices to the boiling water.

Reduce the heat to low, cover the saucepan, and let the spices steep in the water for about 5-7 minutes. Adjust the steeping time based on how strong you prefer your chai.

Add the milk to the saucepan and bring the mixture to a simmer, but do not let it boil.

Once the chai is simmering, remove the saucepan from the heat and strain the mixture to remove the tea leaves and spices. You can use a fine-mesh sieve or a tea strainer.

Return the strained chai to the saucepan and stir in your preferred sweetener. Adjust the sweetness to your liking.

Heat the chai over low heat until it reaches your desired drinking temperature.

Pour the spiced chai into mugs.

Optionally, top with whipped cream and sprinkle with ground cinnamon or add a cinnamon stick for garnish.

Enjoy your comforting and aromatic Spiced Chai Latte!

Feel free to customize the recipe by adjusting the spice levels or choosing your preferred type of sweetener. You can also experiment with different types of milk, such as almond milk or coconut milk, for a non-dairy version.

Hot Chocolate Delight

Ingredients:

- 2 cups milk (whole milk for creamier hot chocolate)
- 2 tablespoons unsweetened cocoa powder
- 2-3 tablespoons sugar (adjust to taste)
- 1/4 cup water
- 1/4 teaspoon vanilla extract
- A pinch of salt
- Whipped cream, marshmallows, or chocolate shavings for topping (optional)

Instructions:

In a small bowl, whisk together the cocoa powder and sugar until well combined.

In a saucepan, heat the water over medium heat until warm.

Add the cocoa powder and sugar mixture to the warm water. Whisk continuously to create a smooth cocoa paste.

Gradually pour in the milk while continuing to whisk, ensuring the cocoa paste is fully incorporated into the milk.

Add the vanilla extract and a pinch of salt to the mixture. Continue to heat the mixture over medium heat, stirring occasionally.

Heat the hot chocolate until it is hot but not boiling. Be careful not to scorch the milk.

Once the hot chocolate is heated to your liking, remove it from the heat.

Pour the hot chocolate into mugs.

Top with whipped cream, marshmallows, or chocolate shavings if desired.

Serve immediately and enjoy your Hot Chocolate Delight!

Feel free to customize your hot chocolate by adding a sprinkle of cinnamon, a dash of nutmeg, or a shot of flavored syrup like peppermint or caramel. Adjust the sweetness and richness to suit your taste preferences. It's a comforting and classic beverage perfect for cozying up on a chilly day.

Golden Turmeric Latte

Ingredients:

- 2 cups milk (dairy or plant-based like almond, coconut, or soy milk)
- 1 teaspoon ground turmeric
- 1/2 teaspoon ground cinnamon
- 1/4 teaspoon ground ginger
- 1/4 teaspoon ground cardamom
- A pinch of black pepper (enhances turmeric absorption)
- 1-2 tablespoons honey or sweetener of choice, to taste
- 1 teaspoon coconut oil (optional)
- A sprinkle of ground cinnamon or turmeric for garnish

Instructions:

In a small saucepan, heat the milk over medium heat until it's warm but not boiling.

In a bowl, mix the ground turmeric, cinnamon, ginger, cardamom, and black pepper.

Add a small amount of the warm milk to the spice mixture and whisk to create a smooth paste.

Gradually whisk the spice paste into the warm milk, ensuring it's well combined.

Add honey or your preferred sweetener to the latte, adjusting to taste.

If using, add coconut oil to the mixture and stir until melted.

Continue heating the turmeric latte over medium heat, stirring occasionally, until it reaches your desired drinking temperature. Do not let it boil.

Once heated, remove the latte from the heat.

Pour the golden turmeric latte into mugs.

Optionally, sprinkle a bit of ground cinnamon or turmeric on top for garnish.

Stir well before sipping, as the spices may settle at the bottom.

Enjoy your soothing and flavorful Golden Turmeric Latte!

Feel free to experiment with the spice ratios to suit your taste preferences. This warm beverage is not only delicious but also offers potential health benefits associated with turmeric and other spices.

Peppermint Hot Cocoa

Ingredients:

- 2 cups milk (whole milk for a creamier cocoa)
- 2 tablespoons unsweetened cocoa powder
- 2-3 tablespoons sugar (adjust to taste)
- 1/4 teaspoon peppermint extract
- A pinch of salt
- Whipped cream, crushed candy canes, or chocolate shavings for topping (optional)

Instructions:

In a small bowl, whisk together the cocoa powder, sugar, and a pinch of salt until well combined.

In a saucepan, heat the milk over medium heat until it's warm but not boiling.

Gradually whisk the cocoa mixture into the warm milk, ensuring it's fully incorporated.

Continue to heat the mixture over medium heat, stirring occasionally.

Once the cocoa is hot but not boiling, remove the saucepan from the heat.

Stir in the peppermint extract. Adjust the amount based on your preference for mintiness.

Pour the peppermint hot cocoa into mugs.

Top with whipped cream, crushed candy canes, or chocolate shavings if desired.

Stir gently before sipping to ensure the flavors are well mixed.

Enjoy your festive and delicious Peppermint Hot Cocoa!

Feel free to customize your hot cocoa by adding a dash of vanilla extract or a sprinkle of cinnamon. Adjust the sweetness to suit your taste preferences. This peppermint-infused cocoa is a delightful treat for the holiday season.

Vanilla Rooibos Tea Latte

Ingredients:

- 2 cups water
- 2 rooibos tea bags or 2 tablespoons loose rooibos tea
- 1-2 tablespoons honey or sweetener of choice
- 1/2 teaspoon pure vanilla extract
- 1 cup milk (dairy or plant-based)
- Optional: Whipped cream or a sprinkle of cinnamon for garnish

Instructions:

Bring 2 cups of water to a boil in a saucepan.

Add the rooibos tea bags or loose rooibos tea to the boiling water. Let it steep for about 5-7 minutes, or follow the recommended steeping time on the tea package.

Remove the tea bags or strain out the loose tea leaves from the water.

Stir in honey or your preferred sweetener and vanilla extract into the brewed rooibos tea.

In a separate saucepan, heat the milk until it's warm but not boiling.

Froth the warm milk using a milk frother or by vigorously whisking it.

Pour the frothed milk into the brewed rooibos tea mixture, stirring gently to combine.

Pour the Vanilla Rooibos Tea Latte into mugs.

Optionally, top with whipped cream or a sprinkle of cinnamon for garnish.

Stir gently before sipping to ensure the flavors are well mixed.

Enjoy your cozy and aromatic Vanilla Rooibos Tea Latte!

Feel free to customize this latte by adjusting the sweetness, vanilla, or milk to your taste preferences. It's a caffeine-free alternative with a delightful blend of warmth and sweetness.

Caramel Apple Spice

Ingredients:

- 2 cups apple juice or apple cider
- 1-2 tablespoons caramel sauce
- 1/4 teaspoon ground cinnamon
- Whipped cream for topping (optional)
- Cinnamon sticks for garnish (optional)

Instructions:

In a saucepan, heat the apple juice or apple cider over medium heat until it's warm but not boiling.

Stir in the caramel sauce and ground cinnamon. Continue to heat, stirring occasionally, until the caramel is fully melted and incorporated into the apple juice.

Once the Caramel Apple Spice is heated to your liking, remove it from the heat. Pour the drink into mugs.

Optionally, top with whipped cream and drizzle with additional caramel sauce for extra sweetness.

Garnish with a cinnamon stick if desired.

Stir gently before sipping to ensure the flavors are well mixed.

Enjoy your delicious and indulgent Caramel Apple Spice!

Feel free to adjust the amount of caramel sauce and cinnamon to suit your taste preferences. This warm and spiced drink is reminiscent of fall flavors and is perfect for sipping on a chilly day.

Hibiscus Rosehip Tea

Ingredients:

- 2 hibiscus tea bags or 2 tablespoons dried hibiscus petals
- 2 tablespoons dried rosehips
- 2 cups boiling water
- Honey or sweetener of choice (optional)
- Lemon slices for garnish (optional)
- Mint leaves for garnish (optional)

Instructions:

Place the hibiscus tea bags or dried hibiscus petals and dried rosehips in a teapot or heatproof container.

Pour boiling water over the hibiscus and rosehips.

Allow the tea to steep for about 5-7 minutes or until it reaches your desired strength. The longer it steeps, the more robust the flavors will be.

Remove the tea bags or strain out the hibiscus petals and rosehips.

If desired, sweeten the tea with honey or your preferred sweetener. Stir until the sweetener is fully dissolved.

Pour the Hibiscus Rosehip Tea into cups.

Optionally, garnish with lemon slices or mint leaves for added freshness.

Stir gently before sipping to ensure the flavors are well mixed.

Enjoy your vibrant and tangy Hibiscus Rosehip Tea!

This herbal tea is not only delicious but also known for its potential health benefits, including being rich in vitamin C and antioxidants. It's a great caffeine-free option that can be enjoyed hot or cold.

Pumpkin Spice Streamer

Ingredients:

- 2 cups milk (dairy or plant-based)
- 2 tablespoons canned pumpkin puree
- 2 tablespoons maple syrup or honey
- 1/2 teaspoon pumpkin pie spice
- 1/2 teaspoon vanilla extract
- Whipped cream for topping (optional)
- Ground cinnamon or pumpkin pie spice for garnish (optional)

Instructions:

In a small saucepan, heat the milk over medium heat until it's warm but not boiling.

In a bowl, whisk together the pumpkin puree, maple syrup or honey, pumpkin pie spice, and vanilla extract until well combined.

Gradually whisk the pumpkin mixture into the warm milk, ensuring it's fully incorporated.

Continue to heat the Pumpkin Spice Steamer over medium heat, stirring occasionally, until it reaches your desired drinking temperature. Do not let it boil.

Once the Pumpkin Spice Steamer is heated, remove it from the heat.

Pour the drink into mugs.

Optionally, top with whipped cream and sprinkle with ground cinnamon or pumpkin pie spice for garnish.

Stir gently before sipping to ensure the flavors are well mixed.

Enjoy your warm and flavorful Pumpkin Spice Steamer!

Feel free to adjust the sweetness and spice levels to suit your taste preferences. This beverage is perfect for those looking for a fall-inspired, caffeine-free drink with the delightful taste of pumpkin spice.

Matcha Green Tea Latte

Ingredients:

- 1 teaspoon matcha powder
- 1-2 tablespoons hot water (not boiling)
- 1-2 teaspoons honey or sweetener of choice (adjust to taste)
- 1 cup milk (dairy or plant-based)
- Optional: Whipped cream or frothed milk for topping

Instructions:

In a bowl, sift the matcha powder to remove any lumps.

Add the hot water to the matcha powder. Use a bamboo whisk or a small whisk to whisk the matcha and water together until smooth and frothy.

Heat the milk in a saucepan over medium heat until it's warm but not boiling.

Add the matcha mixture to the warm milk.

Stir in honey or your preferred sweetener, adjusting to taste.

Continue to heat the Matcha Green Tea Latte over medium heat, stirring occasionally, until it reaches your desired drinking temperature.

Once heated, pour the matcha latte into a mug.

Optionally, top with whipped cream or frothed milk.

Stir gently before sipping to ensure the matcha is well mixed.

Enjoy your delicious and invigorating Matcha Green Tea Latte!

Feel free to adjust the sweetness and matcha-to-milk ratio to suit your taste preferences. Matcha is a type of powdered green tea known for its vibrant color and earthy flavor, and this latte is a delightful way to enjoy its unique taste.

www.ingramcontent.com/pod-product-compliance
Lightning Source LLC
LaVergne TN
LVHW081552060526
838201LV00054B/1867